THE SECRET HISTORY
OF WATER

FLORIDA POETRY SERIES

ANHINGA PRESS

THE SECRET HISTORY
OF WATER

Poems by Silvia Curbelo

Introduction by Robert Creeley

ANHINGA PRESS

1997
Tallahassee, Florida

*This publication is sponsored in part by a grant from
the Florida Department of State, Division of Cultural Affairs
and the Florida Arts Council.*

Cover art: *Eva*, silver print by J. Tomás Lopez, 1989

Cover design by David Pear
Book production by Lynne Knight
Edited by Helen Pruitt Wallace

Library of Congress Cataloging-in-publication Data:

The Secret History of Water, Poems by Silvia Curbelo —
First edition

ISBN 0938078-53-4 (cloth)
ISBN 0938078-52-6 (paperback)
Library of Congress Cataloging Card Number 97-070026

Anhinga Press Inc. is a nonprofit corporation dedicated wholly
to the publication and appreciation of fine poetry.

For personal orders, catalogs and information, write to:
Anhinga Press, P.O. Box 10595, Tallahassee, FL 32302.
www.anhinga.org

Printed in the United States of America
First Edition, 1997

ACKNOWLEDGEMENTS

My thanks to the editors of the following publications where many of the poems in this collection first appeared:

American Poetry Review: "If You Need a Reason," "Tourism in the Late 20th Century"

Berkeley Poetry Review: "Blue Dresses, White Lies"

Caliban: "Birds," "Bedtime Stories," "Spontaneous Human Combustion," "Wish," "Tourist Weather"

Calyx: "Janis Joplin"

Gettysburg Review: "Walking to School"

Guadalupe Review: "Where You Are"

Indiana Review: "Floating"

Kenyon Review: "Tonight I Can Almost Hear the Singing"

Linden Lane Magazine: "Summer Storm," "Photograph from Berlin"

Mid-American Review: "The Lake Has Swallowed the Whole Sky," "Bringing Her Back," "The Secret History of Water II"

Orpheus Grid: "I'm in Love, I'm Floating"

Passages North: "Witness"

Prairie Schooner: "Photograph of My Parents," "Drinking Song," "Dreaming Horse"

Shenandoah: "The Simple Geography of Leaving"

Tampa Review: "First Shift at Hershey's, 4 A.M.," "First Snow," "Last Call," "What Music Is," "River Music"

Verse: "The Death of the Tango"

Willow Springs: "Listening to a White Man Play the Blues,"
"Some Nights You Crank Up the Car Radio and Just Drive"

"The Blackbirds Take Over the Sky" first appeared in *Yellow Silk.*

An earlier version of the untitled piece on page 1 that begins, "A man dreams of a house..." appeared in *South Florida Poetry Review* as "Voices."

"Bedtime Stories," "Drinking Song," "The Lake Has Swallowed the Whole Sky," "Last Call," "Photograph of My Parents" and "Tonight I Can Almost Hear the Singing" appeared in the anthology *Isle of Flowers: Poems by Florida's Individual Artist Fellows.*

Some of the poems in this collection were first published in the chapbook *The Geography of Leaving* (Silverfish Review Press, 1991; Rodger Moody, editor).

I am grateful to the National Endowment for the Arts, the Florida Arts Council and the Cintas Foundation for their generous fellowships. I also want to thank the Atlantic Center for the Arts, La Napoule Arts Foundation and the Seaside Institute for funded residencies that contributed greatly to the writing of these poems.

My gratitude also to the following people for their help and support: Mark Baszto, Meg O'Brien, Pam Rubenstein, Dionisio Martínez, Aubrey Hampton, Susan Hussey, Tom Lopez, Rick Campbell, Helen Pruitt Wallace, Lynne Knight, David Pear, Mark Stroud. And special thanks to Robert Creeley, and to Stephen Dunn, W.S. Merwin, Carolyn Forché, and Rhonda J. Nelson, who read earlier versions of this manuscript and offered valuable suggestions and encouragement.

—S.C.

CONTENTS

III. LANDSCAPE OF TREES AND NUMBERS

IV. WISH

INTRODUCTION

It's clear from the very first words one reads that these poems are fact of a transforming compact of listening and telling. There is a sense of time which is altogether different than the clock's, and the persons are also echoing, archetypal and familiar. It is as if one were moving to what each word itself might tell in the seemingly timeless history of its own witness and invention. Survival is the given. *The difference between then and now/could be wind lifting this page.*

No doubt what we think of as our singular lives is, in fact, a common term, an endlessly expanding fabric which has finally no one thread determining all. It is the insistent story of that reality, that wash of all the others, which sounds here so poignantly—mothers, fathers, sisters, lovers, all the particularizing relations of one's own life that feed both the dream world of memory as well as the waking one of daily acts and recognitions. Water serves them well as a primary, is literally that well which another poet said poetry comes from, "a well deeper than time..."

For Silvia Curbelo the primordial story of human origins in the sea has a decisive counterpart in the physical terms of her own initiating places, Cuba and then America. Both are waking dreams of some echoing beginning, accumulated islands which have been made to ground the facts of a personal life, but also of those shadow lives it must realize are as actual as its own. The fluidity, the melting, transforming nature of this world, is everywhere apparent.

Underwriting everything is the often painful fragility of what a life may then take as its own authority. *Each new breath/is a harbor, then a wave/closes over it / like a book.* Here and now, so to speak, is a curious salvage of all that depends on a past for validation, and the future seems so tender a prospect it can hardly be admitted. Without the least irony or even negation, loss is the absolute condition that being human argues. Again there is a timeless sense. Loss of faith, of heart, of family, of name—but there is no giving up. One moves with one's ghosts of necessity.

Is our world then poised on some flooding alternative, a change we can neither anticipate nor provide for? Who will even prove the "we" of such a statement? We all move, of course, but in the presumption of here and there, "greener pastures." Our world is the habit of such convention, and where we are is where we had thought to be? Not always or even often, as we must learn. *Metaphors are what remain intact,/what are endlessly returning.*

Poetry bears persistent witness, and great poetry is the heart, the fidelity, of recognition. *Faith is/cool water under the tongue,* she writes. *This story is an island.* This art is the way words move together, find company in their own information, sound meaning beyond anything one could ever say.

Anhinga Press is to be congratulated for having inaugurated its series of works by Florida poets so impressively. Silvia Curbelo one must thank for the generous provision of her genius—and for her poems, which have kept such faith with what might otherwise have been lost as well.

—*Robert Creeley*

For Tom and for Adrian.

And for my mother and father.

A man dreams of a house he has not seen in thirty years and something flies out the window. Rain pounds on the brim of his white hat and behind a screen door, behind dark glasses and a yellow scarf, you could be anyone. Say he picks up a telephone. Say he walks home in the rain or buys a magazine or steps into an office building. *Something whispered your name.* A word flaring in space, an animal he cannot track. The only motive is the rain like a letter unfolding itself, *Dear N, The sky is very large, I regret nothing.*

I. EVERY ROAD WASHES CLEAN

When I see dirt washing down the river
Into the gulf,
I think I walked over that ground.
                    —Frank Stanford

*Balseros are Cuban boat people. The word
is derived from balsa, meaning raft.*

BALSERO SINGING

When he opens his mouth
he is drifting, he is
in the air, and the child

he's remembering leans out
of some dark window
in his head. The sunlight

is incidental, falling
all around him like a word
or a wing. In another dream

he is dancing in a cottage by the sea
and music is a language he has just
learned to speak, the cool *yes*

of her throat. The sky goes on
for days with its one cloud waving,
the song lifting him like a sail.

The real boat is lost
at sea, one voice nailed
to the planks of history, salt

on the tongue of 30 years.
A window empties
its small cargo—

an eyelash, grief. Each new breath
is a harbor, then a wave
closes over it

like a book.

FLOATING

When you have no brothers
you are more than you are.
You carry your own flashlight.
Every oncoming storm brings another
blackout and a hot wind you can feel
from way down the road.
In the dark every stone is
an animal. You learn to touch
things without knowing the
difference. *A silverfish
is not a rose, and who wants to know?*
For weeks the rain is one long prayer.
Some nights the river runs to
your back door with its cargo
of bottles, cigarette butts, stones.
You know the places you're falling
towards and how to land there,
how in five years your black hair
will float all the way down
your back. The river is old
and deep. The beautiful crimes
of childhood lift you out of
the water, out of your bed all night.
You touch your small breasts
like a benediction. A tender
rain falls over everything you know.
Your grandfather writes elaborate
love letters to the wife of a dead
president. The envelopes drift
out of his shirt pockets when
you think he's asleep, her name
like a cup you drink from in the dark.

BLUE DRESSES, WHITE LIES

—Cuba, 1962

I remember her face,
the dry cleaner's stepdaughter.
She wanted to sing
but she couldn't.
Her brother smoking in the toolshed.
Her mother dead for half a year.

She'd stand at the window
her arms full of overcoats.
She'd say *Listen,*
the songs on the radio are true.

I fell asleep on the porch swing
and dreamed the empty dresses
came alive, slipped off
the wire hangers, went
to live in my house.
Her mother on the hill without music.
Her brother counting out the days
doing time.

In 1962 the streets were filled
with army trucks.
Teenage boys cradled machine guns
in their arms, their eyes
full of ribbons and numbers.

We'd lie on the bed
listening to her 45s, the words
pinwheeling in the dark,
orphan   cancer   war.

I was six, I was in love,
my favorite song was playing.
She wrote my name
on the soles of her shoes
and watched it disappear.

While dissident poet Angel Cuadra was serving time in Cuba's Boniato prison, his poems were smuggled out of the country inside a guitar.

WHAT MUSIC IS

Nest in the rafters, birdsong,
what the neighbor girl heard
one morning from her narrow bed
dreaming by the book, his own
eyes lifted to the racket of sparrows
in the yard, a sack of marbles
in his pocket, a whole bright
constellation of them, first the blue ones,
then the red. Sun landing on his brother's
boat shoes, the hand-me-down
clothes he wore, looking for his father's
keys, his mother's empty veils, a closet full
of dresses, rose shadowed, humming.

Days spent in the quiet schoolhouse,
landlocked, swimming by booklight, so many
bright fish in the sea, the salty
cupboards smeared with flour, leaving
white footprints on his grandmother's porch,
up till all hours, moonlight hissing
in the yard and a train in the distance.
Writing in window dust, *Te espero, escucha,*
books heavy on his back all the way

down the beach, the satchel light
he carried, the sea at night, every wave
a long road to a morning of boats circling
in the sun, empty, cut loose,

the mother's hum, the widow's wail,
while music wafts all night through the sleeping
house. Branches swaying to the tapping
of rain on a tin roof, heavy as moonlight
rattling the loose boards, cracking
the windows open, what he knew was coming,

the overturned furniture of years,
clocks with their hands ripped out,
still ticking, still alive,

then gone. Doing time in the swampland, road
following the river, becoming the river, turning
brackish along the white stones.
Trail song, wish song,
the bed of light he climbed out of
early one morning in the room where she slept,
the chair where he left her and
the chair where he found her
years later clutching some makeshift
flag, his own torn sleeve.

Then counting the white caps off
Boniato island, each wave
a hand, each hand
a fist, what music is finally
among the gray stones, scrape
of stubble in the prison yard
and a love like felled trees, ghost
kiss from nowhere.

FIRST SHIFT AT HERSHEY'S, 4 A.M.

My uncle climbed out of bed before
the alarm and shaved in the
half dark. He'd stand at
the bedroom sink and let the last
of the night roll off his shoulders,
what was left of the moon,
the mirror looking back.

I imagine him when he was a boy
lying in the tall grass on his
brother's farm and listening
to the first trains going past
like music playing in a distant
room. The rest of his life and
the rest of his life.

In bed his wife kicked
the thin covers to the floor.
I picture him walking towards her
with the straw hat over his heart.
The moon drifting across the
Caribbean. The cold place
where the blade touches the skin.

There are ships pushing off
distant harbors even now.
Cupping the water in his hands
a man knows the hard sleep of
rivers that keep moving and
turn over and wake without light.
Trees remember, stones hold

forth, fish lift the stars
on their backs. Light years before
the first coffee in his mouth

like the first breath, before
the whistle of the sugar
refineries and the hard bread
crumbling down the front of
his shirt, before he wipes
the lather from his face with
the white towel, before the water
in the narrow sink grows dark and
warm when the razor slips, the red
coming off in his hands.

BRINGING HER BACK

Tonight you watch your sister undress
in that perfectly white room
and a memory falls through the air
between you. Beautiful Ana
stepping out of a blue dress.
You were fourteen and you remember
everything. The way the light fell
on her bare shoulders, the dressing table
full of sleep, the names
of the boys she had danced with.

That was years ago, before the last stroke,
before her mind began to go, light
and dark, a constant circling.
She holds the blank mirror up
before the shifting landscape of her face
while you fill in the odd details —
the lake in summer, the white and green
shutters of a Victorian house, the tabby
curled up in the blue chair.

She runs the comb through her hair.
Nothing. The house is wind,
the cat is voicelessness,
pure sleep, an empty place
the color of regret.

 It isn't cruelty that changes
the constant shape of things,
reeling our lives in
one moment at a time.

The way our memories choose us,
tie us to nothing we can actually keep.
An old woman unfolds her handkerchief
to lay that whiteness open. *Remember this?*

You say *cat, house, chair*
working the words slowly through themselves
until the smallest glint of recognition
widens in her brown eyes and she says, *yes,*
yes, I remember, the memory falling
around her like a ruined dress,
a gesture as simple as light
touching a window. The ghosts
of hands pulling back the drapes.

PHOTOGRAPH OF MY PARENTS

I like the way they look together
and how simply her smile floats towards him
out of the dim afterglow

of some memory, his hand
cupped deliberately
around the small flame

of a match. In this light
nothing begins or ends
and the camera's pale eye

is a question that answers itself
in the asking. *Are you there?*
And they are. Behind them

the wind tears down and blows
apart, angel of nonchalance.
The world belongs to the world.

For years he smoked down to the filters
sorting out the pieces of his life
with the insomniac's penchant

for detail. In the heart's
heavy forest, the tree of self-denial,
the bough, the single leaf

like the blade of a word held back
for a long time. The moment
she leans towards him the room

will become part of the story.
The light is still as a pond.
My mother's blue scarf

is the only wave.

II. WHAT MUSIC IS

Why does the water move when it is already there?
—Denis Johnson

DRINKING SONG

In every half-filled glass a river
begging to be named, rain on a leaf,
a snowdrift. What we long for

precedes us. What we've lost
trails behind, casting
a long shadow. Tonight

the music's sad, one man's
outrageous loneliness detonated
into arpeggios of relief. The way

someone once cupped someone's
face in their hands, and the world
that comes after. Everything

can be pared down to gravity
or need. If the soul soars with longing
the heart plunges headfirst

into what's left, believing
there's a pure want
to fall through. What we drink to

in the end is loss, the space
around it, the opposite
of thirst, its shadow.

THE DEATH OF THE TANGO

Ghost of birds flying over.
Ghost of solitude, of a line being cast.
Ghost of the last furtive embrace
and piano notes drifting out the windows
of the Hotel del Lago.
Ghost of the wineglass.
Ghost of the unread letters,
and the violin with its entourage of sadness,
Saturday night with nowhere else to go.
Ghost of the red dress pitched across a chair,
and the blue raincoat with its torn silk lining,
pockets full of sheet music
and postcards from the front lines.
Ghost of warehouses and train stations
and black coffee in all night restaurants.
Ghost of the next to the last cigarette,
Carlos Gardel smoking under an awning
in the black and white rain
with night fading behind him.
Ghost of my father.
Ghost of writing this down.

WALKING TO SCHOOL

Father in a blue raincoat humming
a little aria through his teeth.
My uniform is redemption gray, the color
of old money and overcooked meat.

We're walking past bare market stalls,
past empty bakery windows
and groups of Russian soldiers
milling around in doorways

tossing coins into the air
to see what comes next.
Third grade is repetition
and small mysteries

like working the rosary
without moving your lips.
Walking the streets chewing
on solitude, that odd childhood museum.

Father reaching deep
in his trousers, pulling
a black wing out
with his pocket watch.

It needs winding, so he stops
for a moment and leans into
the task like a man building
something from scratch.

I'm still walking, saying
the names over and over
in my head, an incantation—
Atlantic Ocean, Pacific Ocean,

and the great capitals of Europe,
old tin cups waiting to be filled.

WISH

The difference between then and now
could be wind lifting this page.
The memory of that house rises
like a wave and the world floats up
through its reflection.
I'm walking through weeds and old lace,
the simple furniture of grief.
Metaphors are what remain intact,
what are endlessly returning.
Here is childhood's blue pond,
the apple of sleep. All morning
the light seemed to swallow
all the light. You were wearing
a blouse made entirely of tiny fish
set adrift on a flat blue surface
that resembled the sea.
It wanted to be the sea.
Water is an abstraction
until you hold it to your lips.
The way a kiss belies
its own intentions, a wolf
in wolves' clothing.
In another story an apple dreams
itself into a rose, a pond
retraces someone's shadow
from memory and imagines
any cloud reflected
on its surface is a wave.
Some dreams are both bread
and hunger. Faith is

cool water under the tongue.
This story is an island.
A girl closes her eyes,
simple as an apple,
takes the first bite
like she's never been kissed.

I waited on the docks of sleep
but the ships never came back.
                                    —Kelli Baer

I'M IN LOVE, I'M FLOATING

out of range, I close my eyes
and the world swims into view.
Forget the arsonist
with his book of matches,
I'm a clean pair of lungs,
I breathe and breathe.
I'm in love with cool
surfaces, every night I wipe
the table clean and stare down
the empty plate of years.
I conjure happiness
like bread, I eat.
I'm stupid with the factual.
I memorize the spaces
between words, the cracks
in this story, the music climbing
through a hole in my dreams
until I find myself moving again,
a kind of dancing into place
while the song lingers
like a scent that takes me anywhere,
to libraries and parking lots,
to a strange town, to a room
like this, and here I am.
I chew my books and spit out
the seeds of the unknowable,
such hunger mystifies.

I'm blue and headed elsewhere
like a postcard of the weather
or that old song we hummed
to ourselves as children
to keep the darkness out,
I forget the words.
I'm simple with love, I gouge
hearts out of anything, tree trunks
shudder when I walk past,
the night rushes towards me,
a blind dog cut loose in a field.
I improvise, I lay down
with fireflies and nail my voice
to the first star I see, knife glint
from nowhere. I sleep
and in my sleep I dream
I am in love like this, a bright river
runs through me. There I am
drifting downstream, and there
on the opposite bank
counting my options like black sheep.

THE SECRET HISTORY OF WATER

The body is a stone house   the body
pins you to the ground
crowded with loss   empty
with longing   the weight
of the world falling through it
the way a body falls
fast asleep then suddenly awake   deliberate
in the way it sees you
The body anchored in sleep   suddenly
lifted   suddenly unfurled
a crawlspace for wind   for rain
falling on a simple
city street   the clean map
of your childhood with its hundred
roads back to the leaky house   the room
where you first opened
your eyes saying   *This is the place*
You are the one   until I felt
my hands wash over you   and the glass
of my desire break and spill   water
we could sink through

TOURIST WEATHER

All summer long hurricanes
with the names of movie stars
light up the weather map
across four counties. We drive
in silence out of the hospital
and towards the small strips
where souvenir shops are selling
everything half price.

~

Shells are bones. I've put on
your old raincoat. Whatever
plays on the car radio belongs
to the rain. Weather is the
only news worth waiting for.
Last night the young nurse
threw open all the windows moments
before the first storm hit
and through the trees we could hear
the coarse talk of the waves,
without tenderness.

~

Driftwood, seashell, stone.
Some things are more
than their names.
Like hurricanes. Or cancer.
A word like that can kill you.

~

A shell held to one's ear
tells nothing. Rain
falls between the cracks of what
we mean to say.
Last night I dreamed cool water
filled my mouth and my own voice
adrift inside it
held itself up to you
like any human thirst.

RIVER MUSIC

Let the water rise in you, let it
fill all the spaces in your head, let it
slip through your windows and doors, let it
drench everything you know, the room
and all its ruined voices, the burned out
couches and chairs, the television
always on, let it drag
itself through you
taking the river with it,
its work song, its small humming,
a prayer like an old shoe the current ferries
to the vanishing point, let it
empty itself in you, a kind of thirst,
an inkling, moth of light filling
your mouth with wings, let the gravity
of stones sink through it
for all the sleepless nights,
pink slips, betrayals, the empty
boat of your desires drifting
in a place so deep the land
slips away from its moorings

WITNESS

Someone will be there on that last turn,
someone will drive down that long road
for no reason
or pause in the parking lot of the next motel
holding the cold cup of coffee in her hands.
Call it the law of the land, the only reason
for going anywhere is motion,
because nothing ends and nothing
truly begins, the sky and the sea
are interchangeable and in another town
someone will punch up the headlights
with a used up lottery ticket in her purse.
What's the use of standing still
when everything we want keeps going
and whatever was hovers beneath our lives
like photo captions in a magazine,
This is the sea and what crawled
out of it ten million years ago,
this is the road to Oz, and this
the dulled knife of regret.
And someone will always kick the front door open,
and someone will always push against
that wall of light, the hook and bait
of wandering like another mouth to feed,
because nothing truly ends and nothing begins,
evolution is the wrong number
that connects, is the next face reflected
in the pool of history, the water
we are all baptized in,
and what use is some half-filled cup
when everyone will have to drink?

DREAMING HORSE

I could lie down in all that blue.
I'm watching shadows tell
their own story, a pasture
that sleeps through anything.
The voice is a meadow, the river
is a wing. I wanted
to be there so completely
I thought this poem was you asleep,
your quiet breathing.
The heart is an odd museum.
Sadnesses display themselves
in corners, in rooms
as empty as this field.
The hand denies the face,
the past lingers.
I let my voice climb out
of my cold shoes. It talks
to air, it conjures
what it needs, a landscape
without blame, a room
the color of a whisper.
When I think about love crawling
through this world exhausted
with no place left to fall
I could run circles around
the word. I could say it
to anyone. Listen. Somebody
dreamed this.

THE SECRET HISTORY OF WATER II

The room was a pond with one wave
in it. Words floated to the ceiling
of your voice. The way
you put your hand there
and there, a kind of swimming
out of reason, or loneliness.
I imagined the face behind my face
was more beautiful, an elusive
and more difficult image of myself.
Holding my breath like a child I waited
for storm clouds to pass, for an old
silence gathering behind trees.
Each word cracked open its black shell.
I stared past the moment, past the room,
past the half-open flower of your voice
looking for something solid
to weigh us down, but that could be
torn open, bread or language.
A name spoken in darkness
or a wave: these are words to live by.
I touched you to ease a silence in myself.
Sleepwalking through iridescent skin
the trick is to not quite remember.
The way the hand rocked
by a sudden current lets go
of the branch. The slow drift
out of the center
and the long swim back.

III. LANDSCAPE OF TREES AND NUMBERS

You can't step into the same
River even once
                    —James Galvin

SOME NIGHTS YOU CRANK UP
THE CAR RADIO AND JUST DRIVE

Tonight the moon rises through
the trees like a daughter at her
own wedding making her way awkwardly
through the first dance.
On the edge of town the ancient
fields are picked clean
and the musicians know it,
gathering their instruments,
ordering one more round.
And the baker lost in his grim
wedding cake knows it,
thinking of a girl he met once
in a truck stop, how her face
came back to him for years
like a song on the jukebox
or the threadbare music
of the stars. How even then
she knew it too.
A thin stretch of road
is nothing to a sad man
with a fast car, a dozen
filling stations under
an empty sky. All the young
girls asleep in their dark houses
tired of waiting for the night
to begin. It's a quarter
past ten and the deacon forgets
his evening prayers, thinking
of a young man he knew once

in the army and the last time
he saw him standing outside
a nightclub two miles east
of Saigon. How the memory
comes back to him
in pieces. His hands.
His snakeskin boots. His mouth.

SPONTANEOUS HUMAN COMBUSTION

A telephone rings all night for no one. A trailer door slamming shut. Stars flying up like dust under car wheels. Sleeping in a barn in a windstorm. The letter she keeps in a locked drawer. A soldier kneeling down in the dust under a streetlight. He takes his last drink and he takes his last drink. A screen door blown clear off the hinges. A name like an overcoat thrown to the wolves. The blacksmith and his leather apron. The night shift waiter wiping blood from his shirt. He wants to remember her telephone number. Found money. Hot nights. Looking for the key at the bottom of the well. A letter opener with *Toledo* written across the blade. The moon like a bucket of rainwater tossed over the yard. Heartbreak. White shoes. Stars the size of Cadillacs. If the phone rings don't answer it. The novelist leaning across the bar saying *I wrote the book for the girl*. Smashing the bottle. Starting from scratch. Keeping a promise like a wild dog by a river. Wind blowing through the slats.

THE SIMPLE GEOGRAPHY OF LEAVING

A man stands on his front porch
hoping the crops don't freeze.

It's the last leg of a bad season.
He'd like to walk the feeling off.

This is a story like the first
wheel turning over.

The house is dark.
The wind climbs down.

He moves from room to room.
Every door is a hand around his heart.

Looking into a mirror is a kind of leaving.
He sees himself already coming back.

His wife's soft breathing fills the air.
The bed is still as a lake, and cold.

He could row himself out
with his eyes closed.

He walks out on the porch
just as the first snowflakes hit the ground.

Distance is like a stone beneath the water.
The pieces keep floating up for years.

LISTENING TO A WHITE MAN
PLAY THE BLUES

Pushing the seed into the ground
isn't enough. Whatever blooms

in this place is dumb and blind.
Foreclosure is a one-eyed man.

Nothing falls from a sky like this
except a little rain, never enough rain.

All night my wife looks down
the neck of my guitar

passing the bottle back and forth
like a story she's been telling for years.

So many baskets of hard bread.
You take the shovel to the ground.

The land stares back at you.
The corn drifts towards the sky.

You don't know what dirt is
until you bury your first daughter.

JANIS JOPLIN

There is a song like a light
coming on too fast, the eyes
blink back the static of the road
and in the distance you can almost see
the clean, sweet glow of electric guitars.

Call it the music of the rest of our lives,
a stranger's face peering through
a window, except that face is yours,
and mine. Music like backtalk,

like wind across your heart,
cigarette smoke and bourbon.
Music our mothers must have held
softly between damp sheets,
before taxes, before layoffs,
before the first door closing.

Not piano lessons, not a hymn
or a prayer, or a soft voice
singing you to sleep, but a song
like a green light on summer evenings
after a ball game, after rain,
when the fields finally let themselves go,
and we'd drive past the Westinghouse plant,
past Vail and Arcadia. Music
of never going back.

I'm talking about car radios,
about backseats and hope,
and the jukebox at Pokey's
where the local boys tried

their new luck on anyone
and the real history of the world
was going down, nickels and
dimes, the music floating
at the far end of a first kiss—

the first light of the body
that isn't love but is stronger than love,
because it must not end,
because it never lasts.

SUMMER STORM

The waitress props open her book
against the sugar bowl
but doesn't read it.
She hums along with the hard rock station,
a song about a brittle love
and a piece of someone's heart.

Like a face behind a drawn shade
it has nothing to do with him.
She pours his coffee,
she will do that much.

He stares at his hands,
the coffee cup, the door,
saying nothing. She is beautiful.
When she shakes out her hair
he thinks of water spilling out
or the last moonlight shaking itself
out of the trees.

Could that be thunder
in the distance
or just the music rattling
in his ears? Anyway
he's stopped listening,
even to the radio.

Even the weather station
means nothing to him now.
He knows to sit still
and wait for thunder.
He's got time on his hands.
A good rain is worth a hundred years.

She stares out the plate glass windows.
Pinpoints of light
from the next town are blinking on.
He'll look at her now and then,
but not all of her,
a sleeve, a breast,
a glimpse of hair,
long like the longest night.

Her legs are thick and muscular,
any tree on the side of the road
he could climb. He imagines himself
lost in the leaves
like the pages of some amazing book
and not one word between them.

Can a man ever make a woman
understand the weight of his own voice
lying on his chest? A love like that
takes years, means nothing
to the girl counting out-of-state plates
in the parking lot, keeping time
to the wailing guitars
climbing up towards the roof
where a hard rain is beginning to fall.
He could nail his house
to a music like that.

BEDTIME STORIES
after Marc Chagall

Say it isn't real.
Say this violin is not a window.
The rose opening up from its shadowy heart
conceals its stupid thorn
like a child before his first mirror.
But a painting is not a mirror.
The colors are not real.
The flowers swaying in the hushed light
tell us a different story
and the child drifting through a landscape
of trees and numbers cannot hear it.

The trees are the one constant,
always touching the earth
but reaching for something else.
The violin itself is not color
but lightness. The music
rising beyond the highest
branches imitates flight,
sleep, a kind of floating.
That happens long before the idea
of falling enters the picture.
We attempt to grow graceful and weightless.
We leave our shoes behind.

This is the pure air of a painting
like a child before an open window
waiting for someone to begin
the next story, to bring him
his nightly drink of water
or lay beside him on the little bed.

The bed can be a mirror,
but not as real,
not at all like a painting
or a rose. His head resting
on the pillow is so sweet.
It could never be a tree,
it grows inward, rootless,
floating towards sleep.

Already we know this story
is not real, the colors
are too vague. The child
closes his eyes and imagines
the rest of his life
like a dream about falling
from a great height.
But this is early on,
before sleeplessness, before
he comes to terms with the idea
of gravity and the window
shuts completely in his dreams.
He will lose track of the story.
He will stare at the ceiling.
He will learn to count sheep.

This is a prelude to something else,
something that comes much later,
not sleep, but a kind of falling
through himself in layers,
a sheaf of numbers
adding up to the one belief,
a feeling he can count on,
the pure mathematics of desire.

It happens slowly. He begins to see
himself in multiples of two,
of four, the world unfolding
in a graceful symmetry, two lips,
two breasts, then his own longing
multiplying, becoming
a mirror to the girl
who is beautiful, who lies
in his two arms, who is
like a painting or a rose
or music going on somewhere else.

This happens earlier,
before he learns to think in multiples
of three, before coming face
to face with his two hearts,
the other one that grows
much later, that thorn
leading up to the first kiss,
the first betrayal, the other woman
concealed behind a smokescreen
of desire. These too are dreams
about falling. He falls out of step,
falls short, falls for a woman
the way a child falls asleep
before the story ends.

He has now entered a world beyond
all his calculations. He begins
to count backwards to the first
color, the first sleep, the first
music playing. That happens earlier,

much earlier, before he learns to count
on this completely: Love ends,
stories go on untold
for years, the colors fade
into the background, vanish beneath
the body's clumsy light.

But this is not a painting
he can live with. The trees are thick
and ugly. His own face floats
out of any mirror
like the soul out on a limb,
no longer a child facing an open window
but a man having learned
the weight of dreams.

FOR ALL THE GOODBYES

In a room not unlike this one
someone is always leaving someone else.

Someone blows out a candle.
Someone has finished the wine.

The single glove laid open
on the windowsill tells only

half the story. Try to imagine
the hundred metaphors for flight,

for endings, a door finally closing
and what is left behind—

the robe with its torn lining,
a scarf, cufflinks, an old shoe.

A man's abandoned overcoat
brings to mind train stations,

suitcases, footsteps
vanishing down the hall.

There is no mistaking
the closet door left ajar,

the empty hangers
like the thin shoulders

of loss, of distance.
If you have loved

someone like that
you have imagined his hands

opening other doors, unbuttoning
his shirt in other rooms.

Even as the buttons fall away
there is no turning back.

A dropped shoe is an island.
A scarf will break your heart.

PHOTOGRAPH FROM BERLIN

Memory is the land standing still
for a moment, then a wave covers it.

Snapshots are shields—
what we remember in some way protects us.

In this particular one you're standing
on the balcony of your mother's house
waving at the soldiers passing through.

One of them, a handsome blond,
has caught your eye as he climbs
onto his friends' shoulders
to offer you something, some bread
or a piece of fruit,

his lieutenant's cap
poised over his heart
in a delicate cartoon of love.

Behind you the sky seems to float in all
directions, but the light holds
everything in place.

You cannot know how your life
will measure up against this moment,
your arm frozen in midair.

Your white handkerchief is like a wish.

IV. WISH

Tu memoria está llena de pájaros
—Delfín Pratts

THE BLACKBIRDS TAKE OVER THE SKY

Tonight a moment unfolds like a word
no one has spoken in years.

Someone writes someone's name,
not desire but the idea

of desire taking shape in her mind.
When she puts pen to paper

she touches the skin of a new language.
What is left unsaid opens

huge wings and waits. The way
across a crowded room

a stranger might offer a drink
and we remember thirst,

a door, a window opening in a city
we haven't thought about in years

and beyond it, the thin,
bright air of possibility.

Desire is a stone that opens,
the lovesick heart of every story

ever written. Something
in the way his voice flies out

of his chest, the moment
landing on her shoulder

like a bird. And hope,
that long migration.

TOURISM IN THE LATE 20TH CENTURY

Blue boat of morning and already
the window is besieged
by sky. Grace takes no prisoners
in a town like this. Think of the girl
sipping white burgundy
in the local café, her straw hat
with its pale flower, indigenous
and small as the white roll
she's buttering one philosophical
corner at a time. Even the rain
that falls some afternoons here
is more conceptual, more a tribute
to rain than actual rain falling
on the tulips, a rumor
the wind carries all the way
down the beach.
And would you ask the sea
to explain itself? wrote Kerouac once
in a book about a woman
who was already a metaphor,
rose fading in its glass bowl.
He always knew the world is sentimental,
waving its lacy rags over the face
of the familiar, an architecture
of piano notes and hope.
Imagine the girl, her hat gone,
her bread finished, holding out
an armful of tulips in the rain.
She knows each road leads
to other roads, to small towns
with solid names like *Crestview* and
Niceville where even dust has

a genealogy and an address,
as if there's more forever there.
The tulips long to be metaphysical,
closed-mouthed, more faithful
than the rose. Let the windows
take over. Lean out the small
square of the day, past
the rain, past the idea
of rain, to where the sky
is snapshot blue, the sea
blue by association.

BIRDS

for André Kertézs

The man in the hotel bar thinks
the moon is a camera.
You came into the city like
the rain, believing everything.
The morning sky, for instance,
so helplessly blue and full
of birds. *The photographs
are lies. The photographs
make you remember.*
New England. The girl
with the paper corsage leaning
just out of the frame. The way
some things kept falling
through your hands, shoes,
newspapers, words.
Smoke from your best cigar
in her hair. A place
so deep you couldn't fill it.
All winter long umbrellas
opening their bright wings
all around you. Rain falling
into rain. The city was so
beautiful, a frightened bird
you wanted to touch.
But when you opened your
eyes, her red hair.
The ropes holding the sky in place.
The man in the hotel bar
tells you a story. *In Europe
they hate Americans*, he says.
Smoke drifting slowly across

the Hudson, across the empty
parks, blue as your name,
until you think your very skin
is rain falling over Manhattan.
*The photographs are what has
really happened.* The birds
casting a feeble shadow
on the ground, moving across
the city like a ghost train.
The sky falling dead drunk
into a pond. Sunday morning
you read it in the New York Times.
A child sweeping the sky
into a corner. Laying
the broom beside it.
Climbing the stairs.

WHERE YOU ARE

Because I picture you in a room like this one you are there.
Life is as simple as a photograph, and no simpler. Candles
burning alone in other houses remind me of the world, or
you in it. Other things matter less. A corsage of pale roses.
Any hotel room in south Miami Beach with dirty white
towels like dashed hopes. Absence is fundamental, it
teaches to do without. I am bathing my child, pouring
warm water over her hair and shoulders and in another
country, the black telephone catches its breath. I would
have given this room a different perspective so that the
eyes are immediately drawn to the large window, and in
the distance, a river, trees. The way you pictured it a fan is
blowing the white curtains around, or there's an orange
on the windowsill and that is all. We live alone with our
stories. I am writing to you as if you could walk towards
me out of a room like this one, and there you are, standing
at the bottom of the stairs holding a glass of something
impossibly white, like milk, on a small blue plate. It is the
end of nothing. It could almost be morning.

for Gayle Natale

LAST CALL

I know the man who eavesdrops
at the bar means no harm,
that he washes his hands of what is said,

that if his coffee grows cold
it isn't loneliness.

I know it isn't fear that leads
a beast to water, that sleep
comes down upon the blessed,

that when a good man drinks
the child inside him begins to close his eyes.

I know when the actress lifts her glass
that the movie continues, a role
she has slipped on like a raincoat
but there's no rain,

that in an avenue of trees and
perfect lawns the world is infinite.
The doorman leaning on somebody's
Cadillac loses track of time, his eyes fixed
on the beautiful map of anywhere.

And I know in small towns all over America
the jukeboxes are rigged,
that somewhere a man takes the wrong
woman in his arms and on a dance floor
a love song falls gently to its knees.

And I know the dark begins and ends
in a place we know by heart,
that sleep runs like a river through it,
and sooner or later we are all baptized.

By now the last insomniacs
are gathering their car keys and
drifting home to their books
and the all-night religious channel,

and a voice climbs down an open window
across the dark tenements of salvation softly,
across the silent tract houses,

down among the sleepwalkers whose dreaming
eyes are shut.

FIRST SNOW

In this car years ago. In this
old town. Weeds choking in the fields.
A sky like nothing I've seen. *Close
your eyes.* Every street a new
language. The land empty, land of
birds disappeared, even the sparrows.
Every porch light on Maple Street
still burns for you. I'm wearing
my new coat with silver buttons that
throw little specks of light on
the dashboard. I'm hunched over
the car radio, your sister flipping
through the dial looking for the next
song, for the next window facing west.
In another month she will outgrow you.
I'm 17, I'm falling through the cracks
of myself. The world as we know it.
The first snow of the year.
We drive past Spain's store and past
the high school sliding all over
the road. We turn off 1st Street
and down Twit's hill with the brakes
locked and your sister cuts the lights.
I can hear you laughing.
Your long hair blows across my face
in perfect strands, beautiful
as a loom, the one thing
I want to remember.
Football banners are still tied
to car antennas. Once a year
the Tigers play the Knights.

We're running down the street
making ourselves small to fool
the wind. It's snowing hard.
Down at the Main Tap the boys
notice you first. Your hair falling
in wet strands down your face,
covering your eyes. Every night
a vast landscape. A love song
blowing out the jukebox on somebody
else's coin. So slow. You can almost dance.
It's warm inside but I'm keeping my coat on
on account of the buttons. A row
of orange lights flashes on and off
in the back over the Budweiser sign.
It's the end of October and every
sad pumpkin in the world wears a grin.
Even a fool could close his eyes
and pull a wish out of thin air.
I bum a cigarette from the first
fool that smiles at you and I
take it outside. The snow falling
all over that Ford Galaxie
makes me want to drive forever.
A drunk out in the parking lot
is singing Blue Moon.
Not one star in that sky.

for Laura (1954-1986)

IF YOU NEED A REASON

The way things move sometimes,
light or air,
the distance between
two points, or a map unfolding
on a table, or wind,
never mind sadness.
The difference between sky and room,
between geometry and breath,
the sound we hear
when two opposites finally collide,
smashed bottle, country song,
a bell, any bridge, a connection.
The way some stories end in the middle
of a word,
the words themselves,
galaxies, statuaries, perspectives,
the stone over stone that is life,
never mind hunger.
The way things move, road,
mirror, blind luck. The way
nothing moves sometimes,
a kiss, a glance,
never mind true north.
The difference between history
and desire, between biology
and prayer, any light
to read by, any voice at the bottom
of the stairs, or the sound
of your own name softly, a tiny bone
breaking near the heart.

for Adrian

TONIGHT I CAN ALMOST HEAR THE SINGING

There is a music to this sadness.
In a room somewhere two people dance.
I do not mean to say desire is everything.
A cup half empty is simply half a cup.
How many times have we been there and not there?
I have seen waitresses slip a night's
worth of tips into the jukebox, their eyes
saying *yes* to nothing in particular.
Desire is not the point.
Tonight your name is a small thing
falling through sadness. We wake alone
in houses of sticks, of straw, of wind.
How long have we stood at the end of the pier
watching that water going?
In the distance the lights curve along
Tampa Bay, a wishbone ready to snap
and the night riding on that half promise,
a half moon to light the whole damned sky.
This is the way things are with us.
Sometimes we love almost enough.
We say *I can do this, I can do
more than this* and faith feeds
on its own version of the facts.
In the end the heart turns on itself
like hunger to a spoon.
We make a wish in a vanishing landscape.
Sadness is one more reference point
like music in the distance.
Two people rise from a kitchen table
as if to dance. What do they know
about love?

THE LAKE HAS SWALLOWED THE WHOLE SKY

Some dreams are like glass
or a light beneath the surface of the water.

A girl weeps in a garden.
A woman turns her head and that is all.

We wake up a hundred times and
don't know where we are. Asleep

at the wheel. Saved by
the luck of angels.

Everyone touching his lips
to something larger, the watermark

of some great sorrow. Everyone
giving himself away. The way

the rose gives up its stem and
floats completely, without history.

In the end every road leads
to water. What is left of a garden

is the dream, an alphabet of longing.
The shadow of the girl. Perfume.

THE SECRET HISTORY OF WATER III

In an attic room near a river
a child leans out the impossibly
high window to watch so much
dark water going past.
There is no true color for it.
There is no precise word for it either.
Say *flood*. Say *stream*.
Say *immeasurable thirst*.
You can feel it rising.

NOTES

Pg. 5. "Balsero Singing." Balseros, Cuba's "boat people," have braved the treacherous Florida Straits by the tens of thousands in the last 30 years fleeing political persecution and dismal living conditions. Because they have no access to actual boats, entire families take to the seas in homemade rafts fashioned from inner tubes, tree branches and pieces of canvas and old furniture. Although it is impossible to determine an exact number, it is believed hundreds of men, women and children have died during the crossing. Their bodies are seldom recovered, but their empty crafts often wash ashore along the Florida coast.

Pg. 21. "Drinking Song" was conceived while listening to Schumann's song "To the Glass of a Dead Friend."

Pg. 25. "Wish" is for Joele Renée Ashley.

Pgs. 29, 35 & 71. "The Secret History of Water I, II & III." These pieces are loosely based on a series of underwater portraits by Cuban photographer J. Tomás Lopez, which were instrumental in helping me uncover the thread that runs through this book. (Lopez's silver print, *Eva*, is featured on the cover.)

Pg. 34. "Dreaming Horse." Some of the images in this poem were inspired by Franz Marc's painting "The Dreaming Horse."

Pg. 61. "Birds" was written shortly after André Kertézs' death in New York City. The title and some images and ideas were derived from a short collection of his photographs, *Birds*, published by Mayflower Books.

ABOUT THE AUTHOR

Silvia Curbelo was born in Matanzas, Cuba, and emigrated to the U.S. with her parents as a child. Her numerous awards include fellowships from the National Endowment for the Arts, the Cintas Foundation and the Florida Arts Council, and an Atlantic Center for the Arts Cultural Exchange Fellowship to La Napoule Arts Foundation in France. Her poems have appeared in *American Poetry Review, Kenyon Review, Gettysburg Review, Prairie Schooner, Tampa Review* and many other publications. She is the recipient of a James Wright Award for Poetry from *Mid-American Review,* an Escape to Create Fellowship from the Seaside Institute and the 1996 Jessica Nobel-Maxwell Memorial Poetry Prize from the *American Poetry Review.* Silvia lives in Tampa, Florida, and works as an editor for *Organica Quarterly.*

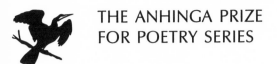# THE ANHINGA PRIZE
FOR POETRY SERIES

*Out of print

RECENT BOOKS
FROM ANHINGA PRESS

This Once
Nick Bozanic, 1997

*Runaway with Words: A Collection of Poems
from Florida's Youth Shelters*
Edited and Introduced by Joann Gardner ,1997

Walking Back from Woodstock
Earl S. Braggs, 1997

Hello Stranger: Beach Poems
Robert Dana, 1996

*Isle of Flowers:
Poems by Florida's Individual Artist Fellows*
Donna J. Long, Helen Pruitt Wallace, Rick Campbell, eds., 1995

*Unspeakable Strangers:
Descents into the Dark Self, Ascent into the Light*
Van K. Brock, 1995

The Secret Life of Moles
P.V. LeForge, 1992

North of Wakulla: An Anthology
M. J. Ryals and D. Decker, eds.,1988

THE FLORIDA POETRY SERIES

When Anhinga Press published *Isle of Flowers: Poems by Florida's Individual Artist Fellows*, we were struck by the number of excellent poets who both reflect and help create Florida's unique ambiance. This state has a number of well known poets whose books line our shelves. But there are just as many fine poets emerging now who we feel merit a national audience. That is why we at Anhinga Press have initiated a Florida Poetry Series. And there is no poet more deserving to kick off our series than Silvia Curbelo with her evocative blend of passion and subtlety. In imagery and subject matter Curbelo's poems embody Florida, as diverse as that concept may be. But a voice as strong as hers resonates widely. Through this series we hope to share Curbelo, and the poets who follow her, with a national audience ever hungry for talent.